I0759789

Mixed into the tapestry of centuries-old architecture, a modern icon rises: *Torre Velasca*. Built in the 1950s, this distinctive skyscraper commands attention with a mushroom-like silhouette that soars more than 300 feet above the cathedrals and domes of the historic city center. The tower's concrete façade and asymmetrical windows create a striking Brutalist presence, yet the design cleverly reimagines the form of a medieval castle. For decades, Torre Velasca remained largely off-limits to outsiders who didn't live or work there, but recent renovations helped open its doors. Torre Velasca now houses restaurants, shops and a hotel, offering the chance to experience this architectural landmark from behind the "castle" walls.

Torre Velasca, Piazza Velasca 3–5, Centro, torrevelasca.it

Milan.

Italy's capital of business, fashion and design. A city that hums with restless energy, drawing ambitious dreamers from around the world.

The country's second-largest city runs on a confluence of contrast. The Gothic spires of the Duomo pierce the sky beside futuristic skyscrapers. Leonardo da Vinci's *The Last Supper* shares the artistic landscape with one of the earliest waves of modern street art. A centuries-old flea market thrives a short walk from the national stock exchange. Storied fashion houses share the spotlight with next-generation streetwear. Through it all, locals from across the city join in the evening ritual of aperitivo, creating moments of connection that bind the city together.

LOST iN connects you with the local voices who define Milan's identity. See the city through the eyes of a visionary design duo. Feel the urban canvas with a street art pioneer. Reframe the familiar with a creative who blurs the lines between commercial and subversive work. Along the way, you'll uncover spaces that shift your perspective: a skyscraper transformed into a vertical forest, a cocktail bar tucked inside a motorcycle shop, a fashion boutique housed in a converted convent, and even a preserved villa that starred in *House of Gucci*.

If Rome embodies the grandeur of empire and Florence the spark of the Renaissance, Milan is the engine of modern Italy. It's where art, fashion, finance, design and dreams all converge to shape the future. Get lost in the creative energy. Get lost in Milan.

Testimonials

Top Five

Our picks for doing Milan like a local, or as close as you can get. Check them off one by one.

Best Bakeries and Pastry Shops

- ☐ Ioste café
- ☐ Pasticceria Martesana
- ☐ Sissi
- ☐ Marchesi 1824
- ☐ Pavé

Best Sunday Lunch

- ☐ Creda
- ☐ Giacomo Bistrot
- ☐ Erba Brusca
- ☐ Osteria Lagrandissima
- ☐ La Latteria di Cascina Nascosta

Best Dinner Hang

- ☐ Silvano Vini e Cibi al Banco
- ☐ Al Vecchio Porco
- ☐ Trippa
- ☐ Trattoria della Gloria
- ☐ Sugo

Best Date Spot

- ☐ Nebbia
- ☐ Horto
- ☐ Altatto
- ☐ Ratanà
- ☐ Langosteria

Best Cocktail Bars

- ☐ Rita
- ☐ Norah was drunk
- ☐ Lacerba
- ☐ MAG
- ☐ Lom Dopolavoro

Galleria Vittorio Emanuele II

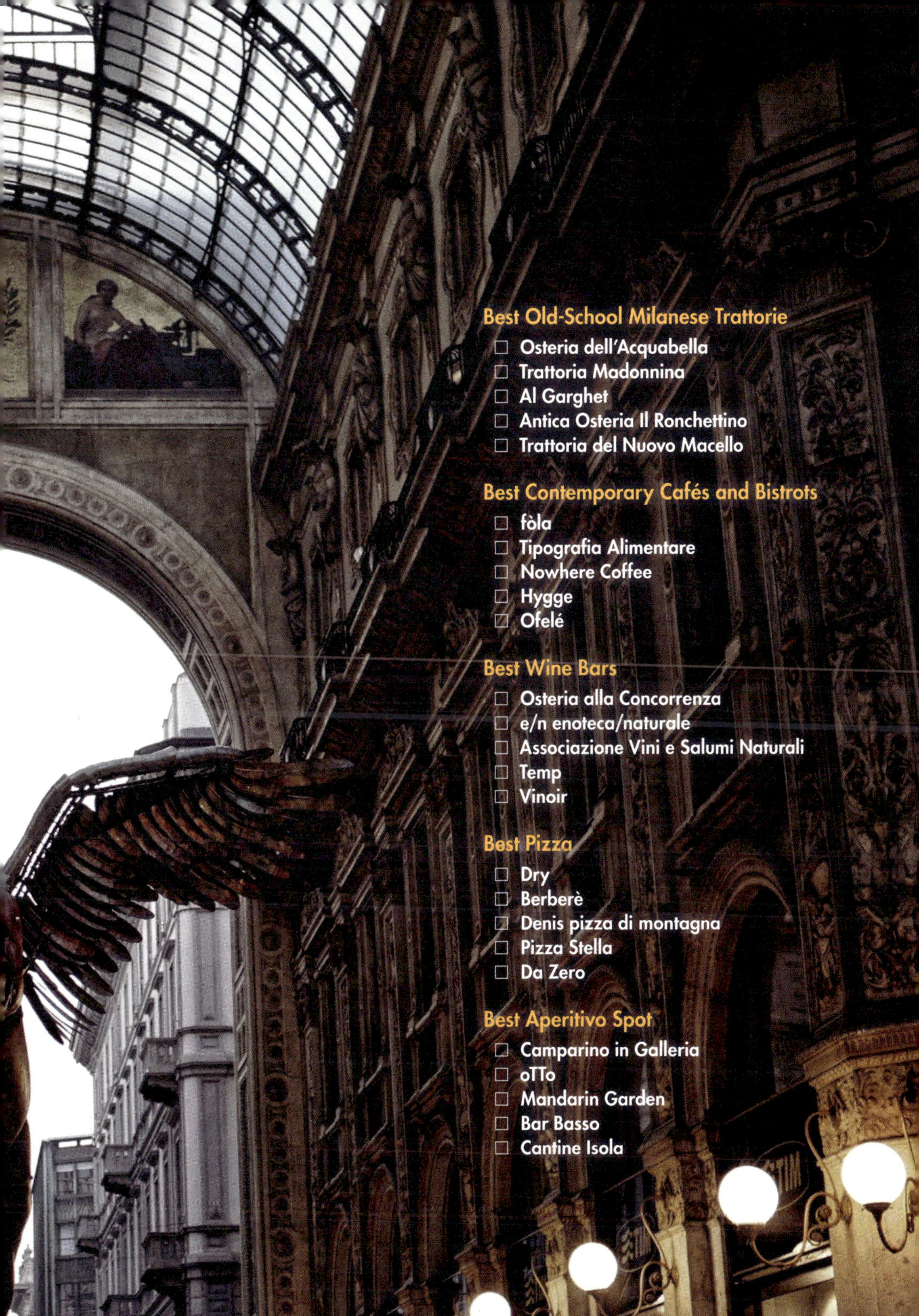

Best Old-School Milanese Trattorie

- ☐ Osteria dell'Acquabella
- ☐ Trattoria Madonnina
- ☐ Al Garghet
- ☐ Antica Osteria Il Ronchettino
- ☐ Trattoria del Nuovo Macello

Best Contemporary Cafés and Bistrots

- ☐ fòla
- ☐ Tipografia Alimentare
- ☐ Nowhere Coffee
- ☐ Hygge
- ☐ Ofelé

Best Wine Bars

- ☐ Osteria alla Concorrenza
- ☐ e/n enoteca/naturale
- ☐ Associazione Vini e Salumi Naturali
- ☐ Temp
- ☐ Vinoir

Best Pizza

- ☐ Dry
- ☐ Berberè
- ☐ Denis pizza di montagna
- ☐ Pizza Stella
- ☐ Da Zero

Best Aperitivo Spot

- ☐ Camparino in Galleria
- ☐ oTTo
- ☐ Mandarin Garden
- ☐ Bar Basso
- ☐ Cantine Isola

Outdoors

Green Spaces & Open Places

In a dense city like Milan, open-air space is pure luxury. The city knows it, offering leafy retreats, peaceful strolls along the canals and buzzy rooftop pools with 360-degree views.

Photo: Ceresio 7

Rooftop Oasis

When the summer heat hits, Milanese in the know head skyward. Designed by Dimorestudio, this retro-chic restaurant and cocktail bar doubles as a city escape, complete with two shimmering pools and panoramic skyline views. By day, rent a cabana and lounge in the sun; by night, the terrace transforms into the perfect spot to enjoy a golden-hour aperitivo.

• Ceresio 7, Via Ceresio 7, Garibaldi, ceresio7.com

The Canals District

Named after the Italian word for canals, Navigli is Milan's bohemian quarter, animated by two historic waterways lined with restaurants, shops and galleries. The buzz along the pedestrian walkways proves Venice doesn't have a monopoly on canal charm. First dug in the 12th century, these man-made conduits served as the city's main arteries, famously used to transport the marble for the construction of the Duomo. Centuries later, they were refined by Leonardo da Vinci, who designed the lock system that made them truly navigable. Trade eventually shifted to rail, but today the revitalized canals flow with life once more, anchoring one of Milan's most dynamic cultural districts.

• The Navigli District

The Original Chinatown

Red lanterns sway overhead as the scent of steamed dumplings and roasted duck pulls you deeper into Italy's oldest and largest Chinatown. The heart of the neighborhood runs along Via Paolo Sarpi, a pedestrian street where Italian façades meet Chinese storefronts. Stop into teahouses, herb shops and design stores, and then taste a surprising fusion of flavors at *Ravioleria Sarpi*. Established in the 1920s by immigrants from China's Zhejiang province, the district has evolved over the decades. Today it's more cosmopolitan, a touch more touristy, yet still a vibrant and authentic expression of Milan's multicultural soul.

• Via Paolo Sarpi, Chinatown

Photos: Sergey Omelchenko, Chinatown; Archivio Orto Botanico Brera

A Jesuits' Garden

Hidden behind a university courtyard in boho-chic Brera lies one of Milan's best-kept secrets. Founded by the Jesuits in the 16th century, the *Orto Botanico* is a lush retreat where rare plants, orchards and seasonal blooms spread across 50,000 square feet. It's as much a living museum as a garden, with centuries of history layered into its shaded pathways. Wander among fragrant flower beds or pause on a quiet bench, and you'll forget the bustle of the city just outside the gates. Bonus: The garden shop sells organic produce and natural cosmetics to take a piece of the greenery home.

• Orto Botanico di Brera, Via Brera 28 and Via privata F.lli Gabba 10, Brera, ortibotanici.unimi.it

Global Styles

Housed in a former 18th-century convent in the 5VIE neighborhood, *Wait and See* is a riot of color and charm, where dresses mingle with home accessories, shoes and jewelry in what feels like an ultra-chic flea market. Uberta Zambeletti, the store's founder and a former design consultant for Missoni, Max Mara and Etro, has a passion for travel that manifests in clothes and objects sourced from all over the world. As you browse, enjoy a cup of coffee, maybe sipped from a La Vita è Bella (Life Is Beautiful) mug, in the recently refurbished shop.

• Wait and See, Via Santa Marta 14, Centro, waitandsee.it

Shops

Your Retail Therapist

Look beyond the glossy storefronts and embrace discovery. Milan proudly rewards explorers with independent ateliers, vintage shops and concept stores that blur the line between retail and gallery.

Calm and Cozy

Pause is a charming and stylish retreat squeezed into 430 square feet of space. Owners Paola and Gloria have created the type of living room you wish you had: chic, relaxed and full of character. A small counter, a handful of tables and cozy booths set the stage, while racks of new and vintage clothing and accessories invite a browse (everything's for sale). Pause doubles as a cultural hub for events like photo exhibitions and as a café that serves wine, craft beer, cocktails and fresh food made daily.

• Pause, Via Federico Ozanam 7, Porta Venezia, pausemilano.it

Photos: Wait and See, Miriam Mongitore @immiristudio, Deus Ex Machina, Nonostante Marras, Guiseppe D.

Motorcycle Diaries

Italians have always had a love affair with iconic bike brands like Ducati and Moto Guzzi. *Deus Ex Machina* (meaning "God from the Machine") is their modern-day temple to custom culture. Inside a quiet courtyard, the space is a dynamic hub where you can find custom motorcycles, bicycles, streetwear and surf gear, all while enjoying a coffee from the café. The establishment is a popular late-night destination, known for its vibrant atmosphere and excellent drinks, with craft cocktails served in unique glass jars. Be sure to ask for a Moscow Mule or a house Spritz with secret ingredients to enjoy a taste of the city's lively *Milano da bere* scene.

• Deus Ex Machina, Via Genova Thaon di Revel 3, Isola, deuscustoms.com

Where Beauty Inspires

Walking into *Nonostante Marras*, the showroom for designer Antonio Marras, feels like stepping into the designer's imagination. Beyond the rack of clothing, the space brims with weathered treasures, including objects gathered on travels, flea-market finds from nearby Navigli and even vintage wooden drawers salvaged by Marras himself from an abandoned needle factory in Piedmont. Though Marras now oversees boutiques across Italy and prepares to open a Milan flagship, this intimate atelier remains something else entirely: a private, immersive world where his creativity comes to life.

• Nonostante Marras, Via Cola di Rienzo 8, Tortona, antoniomarras.com

Alice in Wonderland

Imagine stepping into a friend's home and being able to buy anything you like, from the bed to the bookshelf to the glass in your hand. That's the experience at *Atelier Bellinzona.* Located in a traditional courtyard building, this tiny house and former laboratory is run by Alberto Bellinzona, who welcomes every visitor like an old friend. What makes it special is its mix of styles and the refined taste behind every object on display.

• Atelier Bellinzona, Via Carlo Farini 29, Isola

Photo: Tailetnaner

Pierpaolo Ferrari is a force in the world of art and fashion. As a photographer, publisher and creative director, he's worked with brands like Kenzo, Maison Kitsuné and Campari, infusing mainstream works with his trademark surrealism. As co-creator of *TOILETPAPER* magazine, he's pushed creative boundaries, taking the aspirational visuals of advertising and turning them on their head. His work helped create a new visual lexicon that proves, even within the confines of commercial mandates, that an original vision can still thrive.

Pierpaolo Ferrari

Vantage Point

Milan is a city defined by fashion and design. Hosting four fashion weeks a year, the city draws both world-renowned brands and a new generation of creatives ready to emerge. Within this aesthetic arena, Ferrari is not merely a photographer or publisher but a keen observer of the contemporary zeitgeist. As if holding a funhouse mirror up to the media-saturated world, he blurs the lines between commercial art and subversive commentary. He finds the bizarre in the beautiful, the absurd in the elegant and the deeper narrative in every glossy image.

Flexform campaign by Pierpaolo Ferrari

Villa Necchi
Campiglio
Porta Venezia

Are you originally from Milan?

Yes, I grew up in Milan, and I believe it is a really cool city to live in. It isn't too big compared to Paris or New York. You don't really need a car here, you can just take your bike and go everywhere. Milan is also a good base for work, thanks to the fashion industry. At the same time, the city has a lot of culture that is becoming more and more modern.

What other developments have you noticed?

The city has grown so much since the investments for Expo Milan in 2015. The area I grew up in has radically changed. I like this and hope to be part of this renovation, but I have to confess, I also like my old Milan. If you take a walk at sunrise from Piazza della Borsa to Piazza Duomo, you will see the city as it was when I was a kid.

In one sentence, how would you describe Milan?

Elegance, in which tradition and modernity meet.

Is the city a source of inspiration for TOILETPAPER*?*

Everything that happens in *TOILETPAPER* happens in Milan.

What inspires you most in the city?

The fog in the winter. I love when it's so thick that you can't see further than your own nose.

Where in Milan do you live?

I live in Porta Venezia. This neighborhood is the perfect slice of Milan. It's full of ethnic restaurants and excellent traditional cuisine, and there's a great mix of people living there. It's a real place with real people, so it's a very human neighborhood. There is *Villa Necchi*, from the architect [Piero] Portaluppi, our

Casa Museo Boschi di Stefano
Porta Venezia

Le Dictateur
Porta Venezia

Massimo De Carlo
Città Studi

Archivio Farini
Cenisio

Pasticceria Sissi
Risorgimento

La Vecchia Latteria
Centro

Bar Basso
Porta Venezia

Italian Frank Lloyd Wright, and the museum *Casa Museo Boschi di Stefano*, with its collection of over 300 artworks, including works by Giorgio de Chirico, Mario Sironi and Giorgio Morandi.

Do you have a favorite street in this area?

Via Mozart. I love it for all the really amazing buildings you can discover while walking there.

What is currently the coolest, hippest place to be in Milan?

Lambrate is one of the most interesting areas for art and new galleries.

Speaking of art, is there an image that represents Milan best in your view?

Leonardo da Vinci's *The Last Supper*. This painting alone is a really good reason to visit Milan.

What is Milan's art scene like now?

The art scene in Milan is difficult to describe. There are very few independent galleries and no support at all from the institutions to establish a new, strong generation of artists. Milan concentrates on business and is a very fast city. The art world is more a game of fashion and its foundation.

Is there a Milanese artist that you have your eye on?

Roberto Cuoghi, who lives and works in Milan.

What is your favorite gallery?

Le Dictateur and *Massimo De Carlo*. For opposite reasons, but I think they should do something together.

Are there any underground art venues that you would recommend visiting?

Many. There are some at Le Dictateur and *Archivio Farini*, to name a few.

If you had a day off in Milan, how would you spend it from morning to evening?

Breakfast at *Pasticceria Sissi* where I would spend an hour eating brioche filled with cheese and where I can read *Corriere della Sera*, an Italian newspaper. Followed by a walk to Piazza del Duomo to see an exhibition [at Palazzo Reale or Museo del Novecento], then lunch at *La Vecchia Latteria*. In the afternoon, some gardening and happy hour at *Bar Basso*.

Where do you go to escape from the city?

If the weather is good, I go to the Trebbia River. It's 45 minutes away from Milan. You will find crystal clear water and canyons of beautiful rocks.

What is your favorite season in Milan?

From March to September, Milan is the best city in the world. Milan has long been an established city in the fashion world.

Do you think its importance is still justified today?

I think there are only two cities with the top elegance in the world, and those are Paris and Milan, and this is simply a matter of fact. Prada, Versace and Armani are some of the big brands that ensure Milan's reputation in the fashion world.

What interesting designers and labels have caught your attention?

Massimo Giorgetti from MSGM and Marcelo Burlon. These are talented designers.

Is there a certain style of dressing in Milan?

Yes, there is a classic Milanese style. It consists of the green loden jacket, a double-breasted blazer and leather shoes, like the ones your grandfather would have worn.

[Antonioli](#)
Navigli

Frip
Centro

Creazioni d'Interni
Porta Venezia

Dimoregallery
Brera

Jannelli&Volpi
Garibaldi

Galleria Post Design
Brera

10 Corso Como
Garibaldi

Il Carpaccio
Porta Venezia

Hostaria Terza Carbonaia
Porta Venezia

Da Giannino l'Angolo D'Abruzzo
Porta Venezia

Piccola Ischia
Porta Venezia

Casa Capitano
Porta Venezia

Where do you go shopping for clothes?

Fratelli Rossetti for shoes. Suits and shirts at Prada. I don't do a lot of shopping.

Is there a store that offers up-and-coming designers?

Yes, *Antonioli* as well as *Frip*.

And when it comes to other products, such as items for the home, where do you go?

I love design, and I go crazy for any Fornasetti piece from the shop *Creazioni d'Interni*. I just bought a table from the '60s by Giampiero Romanò, and I could buy everything from *Dimoregallery*, order custom wallpapers from *Jannelli&Volpi* and get a chair by Marco Zanini at *Galleria Post Design*.

What's your favorite book store?

10 Corso Como.

What is your favorite traditional Italian dish?

Polenta, as well as Osso Buco alla Milanese, Risotto alla Milanese and Cotoletta alla Milanese, are my favorite dishes. They are all yellow, the color of the sun.

Where in Milan do you get these dishes?

Il Carpaccio, *Hostaria Terza Carbonaia* and *Da Giannino l'Angolo D'Abruzzo*.

And where would you get the best pizza?

No doubt about that: *Piccola Ischia*.

And pasta?

Da Giannino l'Angolo D'Abruzzo. You will get the best carbonara in town there.

And what is the best pasticceria in Milan?

The best pasticceria for me is *Casa Capitano*. It used to be called Capitano Rosso, and they did the catering when we were on the set for *TOILETPAPER* magazine.

Alpi showroom exhibit inspired by Ron Arad

Artemide lighting through the lens of Ferrari

Art & Design

Visual Narratives

Milan transforms every surface, object and space into an opportunity for creative expression. From a floor lamp that speaks of simple elegance to a vertical forest touching the sky, the city is a visual storyteller that continues to shape the global aesthetic.

Vertical Forest

Milan's cityscape has changed drastically since the 2015 Expo, with rare-for-Italy skyscrapers and bold urban projects reshaping entire neighborhoods. The standout symbol of this new era is the *Bosco Verticale*, Stefano Boeri's "vertical forest" towers, where 20,000 trees, shrubs and plants turn the façades into a living ecosystem that shifts with the seasons. Hailed as a model of sustainable design, the project has won international awards and become a global icon of Milan's forward-looking spirit. By day, snap a few photos, then cross into the Biblioteca degli Alberi (BAM), a contemporary public garden of meadows, groves and flower-filled lawns perfect for a pause.

• Isola, multiple locations, see Index p. 62

Art House

Designed by Ignazio Gardella, the *Padiglione d'Arte Contemporanea (PAC)* is a striking modern pavilion beside the *Galleria d'Arte Moderna* in the Villa Reale palace. Since 1979, it has focused exclusively on contemporary art, hosting an eclectic lineup from Japanese artist Yayoi Kusama and avant-garde musician Laurie Anderson to Milanese photographer Silvio Wolf and performance artist Marina Abramović. True to its avant-garde spirit, PAC has even tackled themes like the impact of glitch art on Italian cinema.

• PAC, Via Palestro 14, Porta Venezia, pacmilano.it

Flamingo Road Villas

For a glimpse of Milan's quieter past, head to the Quadrilatero del Silenzio, a district known for elegant villas and secret gardens. Near Villa Invernizzi, famous for its resident flamingos, you'll find *Villa Necchi Campiglio.* Designed in the 1930s by star architect Piero Portaluppi, this modernist home has been preserved with its original interiors and garden, now open as a museum with a café. The villa even served as Rudolfo Gucci's home in the 2021 film *House of Gucci.*

• Villa Necchi Campigio, Via Mozart 14, Porta Venezia, casemuseo.it

Icons of Design

Milan's status as the world's design capital owes much to visionaries like Achille Castiglioni, Vico Magistretti and Franco Albini. Their former studios, preserved as intimate museums by family foundations, now let you see where the magic first happened. Step into the birthplace of icons like the Flos Arco floor lamp or trace the evolution of La Rinascente's retail concept. Advanced reservations are essential, but you might be lucky enough to be guided by a family member sharing stories that make these places come alive.

• Multiple locations, see Index p. 61

Photo: Alberto Strada

Founded by designers Marco Maturo and Alessio Roscini, Studio Klass is a renowned design and creative consultancy. The award-winning duo has a talent for elevating everyday objects, from furniture and lighting to ceramics and glassware, into aesthetically pleasing products. Their work exemplifies why Italy, and Milan in particular, earned its world-class reputation for product and interior design.

Marco Maturo & Alessio Roscini

New Traditions

For centuries, Italy has been a powerhouse of creativity. Italian artisans upheld this legacy through passion and devotion, but in a world of fast-paced factory production, a key question remains: Can contemporary designers honor this history without sacrificing their independence? Designers Marco Maturo and Alessio Roscini prove that it's not only possible but essential. Their work shows that modern designs can be both timeless and distinctly their own.

Molteni Poldi Pezzoli installation, 2025

L'Antro della Sibilla
Porta Venezia

Ratanà
Isola

Ta-Hua
Stazione Centrale

Palazzo Berri-Meregalli
Centro

You travel a lot due to your job and probably meet people who have never been to Milan. How would you describe the city to them?

Marco Maturo: I list three peculiarities. First, the aperitivo. It's a nice moment to enjoy a drink with your friends, but it is also a good opportunity to meet people and share ideas. I think a lot of business comes out of aperitivo time. After work, people are more relaxed and open to new challenges. Secondly, there are well-dressed people all over the city, and thirdly, Milan is not a big city, but you will never stop discovering it. After many years living here, I still find new spots and new places.

Alessio Roscini: I totally agree, especially in regard to working in Milan. The city has a deep work ethic, with respectful people working alongside each other in a fair way.

Is Milan still a source of inspiration?

Marco: I think the most interesting sources of inspiration for designers are art and fashion design. You can learn a lot from those fields, and Milan offers so much in these two disciplines. The city is full of small art galleries and boutiques.

Alessio: For me, Milan is not necessarily the most influential source of creative inspiration for our designs, but the city is the place to be in Italy because it's the center. All companies have their showrooms here and there are a lot of design events, so it is the perfect meeting point.

What inspires you?

Alessio: We've had the chance to work with companies that have decades of experience in a particular business, and this heritage is a strong source of inspiration for me.

Marco: Milan is often described as the "city of appearance," and at times, this is probably true, particularly if you don't try to get to the essence of the city. The extraordinary thing is that there are hundreds of amazing spots around the city that are not easily found unless you are willing to walk for hours in the right neighborhoods, such as Porta Venezia. Sometimes we like to get out of the studio to enjoy a walk around this area, looking at the breathtaking buildings of the late 18th and early 19th century that are not mentioned in any city guides. They don't scream their beauty, they just exist, and people live in them.

Where is your studio located?

Alessio: Our studio is on Corso Magenta, a historical street in Milan not far from the Duomo. In my opinion, it's difficult to talk about the identities of Milan's neighborhoods. The atmosphere dominating two or three streets can be totally different just around the corner.

Villa Necchi Campiglio
Porta Venezia

Nilufar Gallery
Fashion Quadrangle

Dilmos Gallery
Brera

Luisa delle Piane
Chinatown

Understate
Garibaldi

Italians love their midday break. What do you do for lunch?

Alessio: When you live in a neighborhood and spend so many hours a day in it, at some point you become part of it. We are friends with many bar and restaurant owners. Sometimes we go for lunch in Porta Venezia, where we had our first studio. Most often, we end up having lunch at *L'Antro della Sibilla*, a restaurant founded by two friendly guys from Naples.

Business dinner?

Alessio: *Ratanà* in Isola. It's a restaurant that serves Milanese food inside a great location that was originally part of a train station. You will definitely need a reservation if you want to go here for dinner.

And private?

Alessio: *Ta-Hua*, a traditional modern Hong Kong restaurant just near my home.

As designers, you probably see details in this city that others don't even notice. What do you consider the most beautiful, intriguing spot in Milan?

Marco: *Palazzo Berri-Meregalli*. It's a weird and austere building from the first half of the 19th century. From the outside, it's full of sculptures, mosaics and paintings. This one building mirrors all the architectural styles of the last century, from Romanesque to Liberty, and from Gothic to the Renaissance period. They are all well mixed together. It seems like the architect was a bit uncertain how he should design the building. It's crazy! I like it.

Touch Down Unit by Studio Klass x UniFor (IF Design Award 2020)

Robertaebasta
Brera

Al Mercatino Tra Noi e Voi
Centro

Galleria Rossana Orlandi
San Vittore

Cardi Gallery
Garibaldi

Massimo De Carlo
Città Studi

Monica De Cardenas
Stazione Centrale

Pirelli HangarBicocca
Bicocca

Giò Marconi
Porta Venezia

Pinacoteca di Brera
Brera

Triennale di Milano
Parco Sempione

Alessio: What I like a lot are the big sliding windows of the residence houses on Via Agostino Bertani 10 designed by Giulio Minoletti from 1965 to '70. Each mini-apartment is organized in such a way as to put the relation with the green of Sempione Park in front of the building first. From the street side, you see only a geometric pattern of windows and pillars.

Which place in Milan is the most beautifully furnished?

Alessio: If I think about an ideal interior, I believe the most unmatched one is the house of *Villa Necchi Campiglio*. Its 1930s to 1940s interior was first designed by Piero Portaluppi and then by Tomaso Buzzi.

What about a museum or gallery that focuses on interiors?

Marco: *Nilufar Gallery*.

Alessio: Oh yes, that's very nice.

Marco: As well as *Dilmos Gallery*.

Alessio: And *Luisa delle Piane*.

What is the most inspiring furniture store in Milan?

Marco: *Understate*. The name says it all. They sell unique pieces and products from design brands. If you are looking for inspiration for your home, go there and ask the owner for help.

Alessio: You definitely shouldn't miss the one-brand showrooms of the most famous design companies such as Poliform, Herman Miller, DePadova, UniFor, Cassina and Zanotta.

And if it comes to vintage furniture?

Alessio: *Robertaebasta*. They have a great selection of extremely rare and unique pieces of Italian and French Art Deco.

Are there nice flea markets?

Marco: *Al Mercatino Tra Noi e Voi* is nice. It's a crammed family-run market not far from the Central Station. Go and have a look. You will find everything from cheap plastic accessories to vintage original Artemide or Flos lamps.

When it comes to product design, is there a store in Milan that sells a great selection of nicely designed products?

Marco: Oh yes, *Galleria Rossana Orlandi*. The selection is made by the eponymous and internationally renowned Rossana Orlandi. It's an incredible place. You can go, and after you have visited the gallery, you can enjoy the shop, where you will find handmade plates, glasses, chairs, lamps, accessories, etc.

Where do you go to see art exhibitions?

Alessio: I often visit contemporary art galleries. I suggest going to *Cardi Gallery*, *Massimo De Carlo* and *Monica De Cardenas*.

Marco: I suggest *Pirelli HangarBicocca*. It's a contemporary art foundation, probably the best one in the city. As well, there is *Giò Marconi*, an art gallery in the Porta Venezia area, and *Pinacoteca di Brera*. I like to visit it on Saturdays. You'll find masterpieces of the Renaissance from artists such as Piero della Francesca and Caravaggio there.

Is there a space that focuses on exhibiting architecture?

Marco: *Triennale di Milano*. It's probably the most important design and architecture museum in Italy.

Daily Dose

Invisible Design in the Public Space

Stefano Mirti

We all know that Milan is the capital of design. Is it true? Is it not true? For the sake of this piece, let's assume that Milan is one of the global capitals of design. Design is synonymous with Milan, with fashion a close second and football a third. But for now, let's focus on design. Milan and design. There is Salone del Mobile, the Fuori Salone, the Italian tradition, the masters, the companies and the products, many ingredients, all tied to design. Yes, Milan is the capital of design.

Design is everywhere. Italians ride Vespas, make morning coffee in a Bialetti Moka and furnish their homes with timeless pieces, just because they like them, not because they're masterpieces. And there's one more thing...

In Milan, the most sophisticated designs are in public spaces, so obvious they become invisible. To see and enjoy the finest Italian design, you need only walk around. No shopping required, just stroll, and you're walking through history. The designs are so incredible they disappear into daily life, simply by being there for everyone to use.

Take Malpensa airport. Amid its many complexities, few notice one of Ettore Sottsass' most ambitious projects. To enter a house and spot Sottsass' furniture is exciting, but to have the city's main airport designed by Mr. Memphis himself is another level. So far beyond, in fact, that 99 percent of stressed travelers don't even notice it. Malpensa Terminal 1, not to be confused with the newer wings, was designed by Sottsass Associati at the peak of their influence in 2000. An airport by Norman Foster or Renzo Piano would be expected. A postmodern one? Unique.

Prefer postmodern airports? Head to Linate, where Aldo Rossi worked on the extension between 1991 and 1993. Less powerful than Malpensa, but still impressive, especially when viewed from the landing strips.

Or take the subway, linea rossa (red) or linea verde (green). If Ettore Sottsass was the king of postmodernism, Franco Albini was the knight of Italian modernism. In one of the stations, take a break and stop for a moment. Pause in one station and notice the details: handrails, color palettes, surfaces and signage. Together they form a universe built between 1962 and 1969, a collaboration between Albini and Franca Helg, with graphics by Bob Noorda. The Metropolitana is one of Albini's masterpieces: more than 50 years old, yet still timeless, and all the more fascinating with age.

Want something tougher? Ride the passante urban train and get off at Rogoredo or Certosa. Angelo Mangiarotti designed much of the passante in the 1980s, including Bovisa, Repubblica and Porta Venezia. But Rogoredo and Certosa are standouts, where engineering, architecture and product design merge seamlessly. Rho-Pero station (2006) is one of his last works.

Other examples abound. Stazione Centrale, by Ulisse Stacchini, opened in 1931 and defies easy categorization with a monumental blend that looks almost Mesopotamian. Or go back further, to Leonardo da Vinci's Navigli canal system. Though much is gone, remnants remain around Via San Marco.

The list could be longer, but this is a start. What's striking is that Milan offers so much "design for all," with public design tied

Linea Rossa designed by Franco Albini, a fine example of 1960s Italian design

to function. Italy often stages itself theatrically, where form follows form: palazzi, piazze, the *dolce vita* of sipping an aperitivo at sunset.

Milan is different. Function is in its DNA. Design here is found in train stations, airports, subways, even gas stations. Yes, Milan has its palazzi, but it also has places, objects and systems where function consumes form and becomes pure meaning.

Speaking of gas stations, check out Piazzale Accursio, where Mario Bacciocchi designed a jewel for Agip between 1951 and 1953.

Milan is home to some of the finest design. Because it serves function first, we often overlook it, at least until it ages, like the yellow trams still rattling through the streets. Officially ATM Class 1500, or Type 1928, they've been running since their namesake year. Nearly a century later, they're still at work.

Stefano Mirti is an architect, designer and teacher. Founder of IdLab, Milan. Together with Susanna Legrenzi, he was the head of the social media team for Expo Milan 2015. He teaches at Bocconi business school in Milan. Head of Relational Design on-line/off-line master (Abadir, Fine Arts Academy Catania). For many years, he has been working on new forms of teaching: Whoami, Design 101, Architecture 101 and several other projects.

Everyday Elegance

A photo showcase by Stefan Giftthaler

Stefan Giftthaler shoots for publications like *Vogue* and *Icon*, but he furthers his artistic expression by taking fresh looks at familiar spaces. In collections like “Milan’s Surfaces” and “Swimming Pools in Milan,” the photographer showcases the city’s hidden aesthetics and the elegance of everyday life. Here’s a look at Milan through Giftthaler’s lens.

PARRUCCHIERE ELEGANTE

Comune di Milano
passo
carrabile

11
12

FIAMM
BATTERIE
TROMBE
FERRARI FOREVER
FORMULA 1
ELETTRAUTO
CERQUONI
MILANO
DENSO
HONDA
DENSO
McQUEEN
CASSA
MARCHESI

Andrea Caputo

Urban Explorer

Andrea Caputo is an Italian architect making waves on the international design scene. He's the creative force behind striking designs for Carhartt WIP stores in Lisbon, Moscow and Seoul, as well as the Retro Super Future flagship store in New York City. Beyond his architectural work, Caputo is a respected curator and editor. He's explored global graffiti culture in his book *All City Writers* and served as editor for *Public Domain: The Tunnel Issue*, which examined the complex relationship between public and private spaces.

For Andrea, Milan isn't just a city of buildings, it's a living canvas. Rooted in street art and urban culture, he urges visitors to skip rigid tours and instead lose themselves in its streets. Milan, he says, is best discovered on your own terms: a city where hidden gems reveal themselves as you wander.

Museo del Novecento
Centro

How did you get into publishing and architecture?

During the mid-nineties, I applied to a graphic design school in Milan. I was interested in established authors like Neville Brody, Bruce Mau, Ken Garland and other names from Europe like M/M Paris. Back then, architecture was just a good way for me to escape obligatory military service. With a couple of exams per year, it was possible to postpone the army. Graphic design school wasn't recognized as an "official" diploma, so architecture became my semestral handicap, slowing my other interests. I still remember Giovanni Denti, a great professor at Politecnico, obsessed with the essay "Ornament and Crime" by the Austrian architect Adolf Loos, my first architectural spark. Aside from that, I was still very involved in the European graffiti scene, taking part with actions and in fanzine publishing. Self-publishing, and mostly self-distribution, was the best way to travel and keep tight connections with partners all over Europe and the United States. I guess interrailing kept many youth cultures' networks tight, giving me the chance to sleep on trains, visiting 10 to 20 cities per month and so on.

What distinguishes this city from others?

I don't see a big cultural or urban gap between Milan, Siena, Paris or Seoul. What distinguishes cities resides more in how you approach them. It is in the visitor's gaze. Milan is peculiar compared to other Italian cities. It seems to be permanently changing. It has its deep Italian roots, but they are linked to a very international vision. These unique characteristics make it resemble other European and worldwide cities more than other Italian cities.

What are the best things in the city for you?

There is the *Museo del Novecento*, which was renovated by the architect Italo Rota. I would say every project by Italo Rota is worth a visit, but this particular project is a personal favorite. Everyone should find out what the best thing in Milan is on their own. The city offers food for every taste. You can just walk through certain quarters and experience the life of the town.

Where can I discover some hidden architectural highlights?

In winter, there's a sort of magic pervading the land between each condo, like small green plots with English grass, fog and nothing else. Another place worth discovering is Vicolo delle Lavandaie, a tight alley with a river in the middle. It's a place where women used to do laundry in centuries past, located just next to Navigli, a young area and the center of nightlife. You can take beautiful walks there during the day. Another area that you would not expect to find in Milan is Villaggio dei Giornalisti, a district in the north with elegant Liberty-style houses and strange buildings, such as igloo houses. Here you can take nice architecturally stimulating walks and breathe in the real life of the city.

Talking about different areas, which are the most interesting city districts for you?

I think that Lambrate district is experiencing a peculiar moment. It has become a district for the creative industry, with architectural offices and design galleries. A place where young people can develop their unconventional ideas, outside the main and academic streams. The area has moments of great success and booms with visitors during Design Week, when people

Un Posto a Milano is located in Cascina Cuccagna, a colonial house surrounded by a huge park.

Lux Bar
Stazione Centrale

ONEOFF
Precotto

Long Chang
Chinatown

The Manhattan
Garibaldi

Piscina Cozzi
Repubblica

come for the numerous organized events. This is at the same time as the Salone del Mobile, the Milan Furniture Fair, which is always worth a visit.

Milan in 38 hours—what are your recommendations?

Start with breakfast in Stazione Centrale at *Lux Bar*. Then pay a visit to *ONEOFF*, an architectural prototype lab in Precottoi. For lunch, I would recommend the Chinese trattoria *Long Chang* in the Paolo Sarpi area. After that, pause for a coffee or cocktail at *The Manhattan*. If you are interested in architecture, go for a short afternoon swim at *Piscina Cozzi*. It's a great way to see the amazing design of the space. You could then go for an aperitif at *Santeria Paladini 8*. If you like to sit back and observe life in the city, go to *Pizzeria Mundial* in Piazza Bottini. Since all of this is quite affordable, I suggest investing your daily budget at *Osaka* restaurant in Corso Garibaldi. These are all very personal recommendations and may be more of a list of intimate places, perhaps not interesting for tourist

Santeria Paladini 8
Lambrate

Pizzeria Mundial
Citta Studi

Osaka
Garibaldi

Pavè
Porta Venezia

Pirelli
HangarBicocca
Bicocca

Un Posto a Milano
Porta Romana

Deus Ex Machina
Isola

Moroni Gomma
Centro

Galleria Rossana
Orlandi
San Vittore

Upcycle
Lambrate

Triennale di Milano
Parco Sempione

purposes. An alternative plan could be breakfast at *Pavè* on Via Casati and a visit to *Pirelli HangarBicocca*. You can follow that with a traditional Italian lunch at *Un Posto a Milano*, a farmhouse-turned-restaurant in Porta Romana. After lunch, you might be ready for some shopping in one of the diverse fashion streets of Milan, such as in the historic Ticinese area. The *Deus Ex Machina* store is of interest for unique fashion finds.

What are your top three stores currently?

Moroni Gomma is a very nice design store where you can find things that you just can't get anywhere else. *Galleria Rossana Orlandi* has two floors and winds around a green courtyard. Here you can find vintage and contemporary furniture. Their gallery showcases unique pieces from young designers from around the world.

If you take a rest, where do you feel most at peace?

In my office, but it's a private place. I would suggest *Upcycle*, an urban bike café. It's a place where I can work, have meetings or just sit and enjoy a coffee in an unconventional place, namely an abandoned bike garage. Another option, for a sunny day, is Parco Sempione, the largest public park in Milan. You can walk or lie in the grass and rest. Within its premises, you'll also find the 14th-century Castello Sforzesco. There's also the *Triennale di Milano*, a museum built on the edge of the park. During summer months, the sculpture garden is open. The bar is also a nice place to hang out.

Coming back to your profession, if you were to do a forecast of what Milan's architecture of tomorrow looks like, what would you say?

My guess is it will remain very private. Major parts of the city—enormous city blocks, if not entire neighborhoods like Bicocca and Fiera—are developed independently from citizens, municipalities and public debate. They are developed architecture. New and random islands in the city. I don't see this as a 100 percent negative consequence. These varieties enrich the city and its inhabitants. I feel the same about the expansion of the subway-linked districts that are distant from each other in geographical and architectural terms and for suburbs to be requalified and redeveloped.

Bites

Fashionable Feasts

Food is a way of life in Milan, and the city invites you to start living it. Pull up a chair at a classic trattoria, wander through food markets and taste the city one bite at a time.

A Casual Affair

While its original namesake is famous for fish, *Giacomo Bistrot* offers a more relaxed, meat-focused experience. True to its bistro style, the menu moves quickly from hearty plates to seasonal indulgences like fresh oysters and truffles that pair brilliantly with a glass of champagne or fine wine. The setting mixes Paris and London: tightly packed tables in classic bistro fashion and walls lined with leather-bound books like an old British library. Open until midnight every day, it's a go-to spot for a late-night dinner.

• Giacomo Bistrot, Via Pasquale Sottocorno 6, Risorgimento, giacomomilano.com

Lunch Break

For an authentic taste of Milanese life, slip into *Giannasi 1967* on a Saturday afternoon and join the locals queuing for lunch. This beloved food kiosk dishes up Italian comfort food like lasagna, Sicilian arancini, cannelloni and a creamy Risotto alla Milanese, but the star is, and always has been, the roast chicken. What began as Dorando Giannasi's humble poultry shop has become a city institution, thanks to a recipe that hasn't changed in more than 50 years. Each bird is marinated for 24 hours and then slow-broiled until it's impossibly tender and fragrant. It's comfort, tradition and Milan all on a paper plate.

• Giannasi 1967, Piazza B. Buozzi 2, Porta Romana, giannasi1967.com

Nordic Vibes

Røst is a hip, Nordic-inspired bistro and one of Milan's most exciting modern restaurants. Here, culinary tradition is reimagined with care, not shock value. The menu is short, seasonal (with a strong farm-to-fork approach) and intentionally unstructured. It puts flavor before formality and encourages a more intuitive, shared dining experience. It's a formula that feels fresh but familiar, modern yet warm, hyper-local but never predictable, creative without trying too hard. The interiors echo the ethos: clean-lined and inviting, leaning on the minimalist. Order a few plates to share, and let the staff guide you through their smart list of natural wines.

• Røst, Via Melzo 3, Porta Venezia, rostmilano.com

Classic Comforts

Isola has no shortage of great places to eat. For a classic Milanese meal, though, *Osteria dal Verme* is hard to beat. Rustic interiors set the tone—think exposed brick, wooden tables, wicker lamps—paired with warm, friendly service and a menu full of northern Italian comfort food, including Risotto alla Milanese, polenta taragna with toma cheese and black truffle, and more. The wine list leans heavily toward Italian reds, perfect for washing it all down.

• Osteria dal Verme, Via Jacopo dal Verme 19, Isola, osteriadalverme.it

Taste of the Town

Locals joke that you need to take a day off to properly experience *Trattoria de Nuovo Macello.* The ambiance charms you with a rich sense of heritage, but the real magic happens when the plates arrive, as each dish strikes a masterful balance between rustic charm and refined elegance. True to its name ("New Slaughterhouse"), Nuovo Macello found new life under fresh ownership in 1959. Now in its third generation of family stewardship, the restaurant honors tradition while embracing culinary creativity. The Veal Cotoletta alla Milanese lives up to every expectation that's implied in the Nuovo Macello name, but be sure to save space for their legendary gorgonzola gelato.

• Trattoria del Nuovo Macello, Via. Cesare Lombroso 20, Porta Vittoria, trattoriadelnuovomacello.it

Identità Milano

Housed in a beautifully restored industrial building, *Ratanà* brings warmth and history to the futuristic landscape of Porta Nuova. Led by chef Cesare Battisti, it has become one of Milan's most celebrated dining addresses, famed for a risotto that ranks among the city's very best. With a kitchen dedicated to sourcing the highest-quality ingredients, this is Milanese cuisine at its finest.

• Ratanà, Via Gaetano de Castillia 28, Isola, ratana.it

Working-Class Kitchen

Trattoria da Tomaso is the definition of family-run: the son in the kitchen, the father on the floor, the mother at the coffee and cash. Dad may look a little gruff, but only because he's always in motion as this place is perpetually full, especially with local workers. After 1pm, getting a table can be tough. Forget fine crystal and silverware. Here, it's all about honest Italian cooking and prices that feel like they're from another era.

• Trattoria da Tomaso, Via Gaetano de Castillia 20, Isola

Market Bites

For a casual taste of the neighborhood, *Mercato Isola* offers a lively mix of quick bites and diverse flavors. With more than 80 years of history, this market in Piazzale Lagosta has been recently transformed into a small gastronomic hub, home to delicatessens, wine shops—we recommend Celeste al Mercato for natural wines—and standout kitchens like Katsusanderia, where pillowy milk-bread sandwiches are stuffed with crisp, golden katsu. You'll find everything from fresh pasta to matcha waffles, making it the perfect spot to graze your way through an afternoon.

• Mercato Isola, Piazzale Lagosta 7, Isola, @mercatoisola

Simmer Up

Non Solo Lesso is about much more than the hearty meat stew that inspired its name, which translates as "not just boiled meat." The menu celebrates Lombardy and Piedmont traditions, with dishes like beef braised in red wine for two days before a slow, hours-long cook. Run by the same family for three generations, the restaurant feels like an Italian home, where guests of all ages gather around wooden tables to eat and drink together.

• Non Solo Lesso, Corner of Via Giorgio Jan and Via Francesco Redi, Porta Venezia, nonsololesso.it

46
ARTO

A stalwart of Italian street art, Mr. Wany (real name Andrea Sergio) has spent more than three decades moving fluidly between roles: illustrator, advertising graphic designer, art director, screen printer, self-publishing editor, b-boy and occasional tattoo artist. Dedicating himself fully to contemporary art since 2006, he founded both The Amazing Art studio in Opera, Milan, and Amazing Day, Italy's longest-running free festival of art, music and dance. With a rich background in the visual arts and an instinctive flair for color, he has explored every stage of lettering and far beyond.

Mr. Wany

Milan Gives, Milan Takes

Milan's streets are alive with art. Across neighborhoods, there are murals, paste-ups, tags and entire façades that double as open-air galleries, showcasing everything from portraits and cityscapes to local hero tributes and flashes of pure abstraction. Over the past two decades, the city has grown into one of Europe's most dynamic hubs for street culture, where international names rub shoulders with homegrown talent. Among the latter, few figures stand taller than Mr. Wany. From large-scale murals to his long-running festival Amazing Day, he has helped shape not only Milan's visual landscape but also its reputation as a stage for global street art.

Fondazione Prada
Porta Romana

Pirelli
HangarBicocca
Bicocca

Fabbrica del Vapore
Chinatown

PAC (Padiglione d'Arte Contemporanea)
Porta Venezia

Triennale Milano
Parco Sempione

Mudec (Museo delle Culture)
Tortona

Museo Archeologico
Corso Magenta

Galleria d'Arte Moderna (GAM)
Porta Venezia

Museo della Scienza e della Tecnologia
San Vittore

WAG

How did you arrive in Milan and what made you stay?

I came to Milan in 2006, after the *Street Art Sweet Art* exhibition at the PAC, because I had started a full-time collaboration with a gallery. Before that I worked in Bologna, studied in Rome and was born in Brindisi. At that time, Milan was the right place for anyone who wanted to grow artistically, breathe new influences and have more opportunities. I stayed because I found fertile ground here. Milan is a city that stimulates you, tests you constantly and always offers something new, even if not always in a positive way.

What's the most significant change you've seen in the city since living here?

A greater awareness of our work and our role in society. At one time we were seen as public enemies, almost the "bad guys." Now we're also considered artists who launch messages and inspire generations of young people. The truth, as often happens, lies somewhere in the middle. Our work isn't just painting. It's also political and social, branching into areas that aren't always easy to understand or even always legal.

What does Milan represent to you?

Milan is like the Duomo: a Gothic jewel, fascinating, but full of sharp spires and monstrous statues hiding behind sacred images.

If you had to describe Milan in one phrase?

"Milan gives, Milan takes!" Just like the street. A kind of Tao, a mantra that always comes back.

Which neighborhood do you love most and why?

More than places, I'm tied to memories: Barona, Navigli, Via Tortona, Via Torino, Chinatown… neighborhoods destroyed and regenerated many times. I approach the center and the suburbs in the same way, though the suburbs feel closer to who I am.

Is there a place, or places, that inspire you in the city?

Industrial spaces: old warehouses, abandoned areas. They tell stories. Often I've found the right energy to create in that atmosphere of industrial decline that Italy, and Milan in particular, captures so well.

When you travel abroad, what do you miss most about Milan?

My family. In recent years I've chosen to travel less, but starting in December, after publishing my first monograph, I'll be on the road non-stop throughout 2026.

Which galleries and museums do you consider must-sees?

Too many to list, but definitely *Fondazione Prada*, *HangarBicocca*, *Fabbrica del Vapore*, *PAC*, *Triennale*, *Mudec*, the *Archaeological Museum*, *GAM* and the *Museum of Science and Technology*. And I'd add the independent galleries, as they give space to more experimental languages.

Tell us about Amazing Day. What is it, how was it born and how has it evolved?

Amazing Day is a street culture festival that began as a hip-hop jam in 2006 in Bologna, created as a chance to meet friends from across Italy and abroad in one "amazing" day. Over time it grew into what it is today: Italy's longest-running free cultural festival, mixing art, dance, music and more. In recent years it moved to Milan and its outskirts, like Molino Dorino, Pero, Navigli, Opera and Locate di Triulzi. It's always been and will always remain free. Street culture shouldn't be exclusive, but as

Centro

Astrofat
Bande Nere

The Amazing
Art Studio
Opera

inclusive as possible. With the support of the Comune di Locate di Triulzi, the Arti e Mestieri Sociali cooperative and sponsors, we manage, though not without effort, to cover the costs for an event that now attracts around 3,000 visitors over three days.

A project in Milan you're especially proud of?

There are many. In 2008, I painted what was probably Milan's first advertising façade for Nike in Porta Genova, back when it wasn't a trend like it is now. I painted my Kabuki Rose at the *Focus* editorial offices, and I designed the Rozzano façades project in 2020. I've painted countless walls with Milan crews, held exhibitions and lived through countless night adventures.

One of the most meaningful things was when my friends Daniel and Marco Materazzi convinced me to start tattooing. For a while I had the chance to tattoo artists I admire, like Clementino and my friend Jesto, who sadly passed away in August 2025.

Where should someone go in Milan to discover street art?

Milan is full of it: street art, writing, poster art, sticker art, murals, guerrilla marketing, even fake brand façades, all the way to the hardest vandal tags on churches. For my own projects: Rozzano, where I worked with Hunto and Vesod on unique new muralism pieces for the community. Or the walls near the iron bridge on the Navigli at Viale Cassala and Via Malaga, painted during Amazing Day, which was tough but rewarding. And of course Locate di Triulzi, the historic site of so many editions, where thousands of international artists, from the US, Russia, South America, Australia, New Zealand, Europe, the UK, Serbia, Switzerland and Japan, have painted.

How would you define Milan's art scene today?

There are very talented artists in different disciplines, recognized internationally, and plenty of "wannabes." There's confusion, especially in communication. Agencies and media often can't tell who's posturing from who's truly creating. With big money in the mix, that becomes a self-goal for brands, collectors and investors. Sadly, even some galleries fall into this confusion, selling bad work from unknowns as if they were "kings of street art."

Shops you'd recommend for street culture lovers?

Several. *WAG* is definitely the most historic. *Astrofat* is one I frequent and collaborate with. And then there's my own project, *The Amazing Art Studio* in Opera, tied to *theamazingart.com*, my e-commerce platform. We support small editorial productions like *Ill Fame Magazine*, born in 1996 as an underground fanzine, and capsule collections in limited editions by international artists, including myself.

For you, Milan is...

Milan is challenge and opportunity. A city that gives you nothing for free, but if you live it the right way, it can give back so much.

Upcoming projects?

I am set to release my first monograph, *Mr. Wany—Since 1990*, in December [2025]. Three volumes in a box set, about 600 pages covering my entire creative journey to date. A limited edition of 600 copies is already on preorder via theamazingart.com, with a collector's edition of 100 signed and hand-painted box sets also coming soon.

Raising the Bar

Milan's drinking culture honors its past while embracing the future. Between legendary cocktail spots, mysterious speakeasies and a world-famous jazz club, Milan invites you to pull up a stool and savor the moment.

Glasses Up

Most evenings in Porta Venezia start at *Bar Picchio*, a lowkey bar that's a bit of an institution in the neighborhood, not least for its unpretentious vibes, honest prices and the fact that it's been around since 1969. Come for aperitivo, and you might find yourself perched on the sidewalk, elbow-to-elbow with fellow patrons, all sharing the same stretch of pavement over spritzes and snacks. Across from it, *Osteria alla Concorrenza* (photo) is another top spot for a drink, though here, it's wine and nothing but. Opened by chef Diego Rossi—the man and mind behind Trippa, one of Milan's most sought-after neo-trattorie—it's a retro-looking enoteca with an extensive selection of bottles and a menu of humble dishes to pair with your vino, from focaccia with mortadella to caponata.

• Porta Venezia, multiple locations, see Index p. 64

Phoney Negroni

A true Milanese institution, *Bar Basso* is famous for two things: being the first bar in Milan to introduce the aperitif concept to everyday people and for inventing the Negroni Sbagliato. This signature cocktail, a happy accident of a bartender who mistook prosecco for gin, is served on the rocks in huge, dramatic glasses. While it remains a beloved local watering hole, the bar is also a major draw for the international design crowd, especially during Salone del Mobile. Come and enjoy cocktails at the counter with olives, nuts and chips, the way it's been done for years.

• Bar Basso, Via Plinio 39, Porta Venezia, barbasso.com

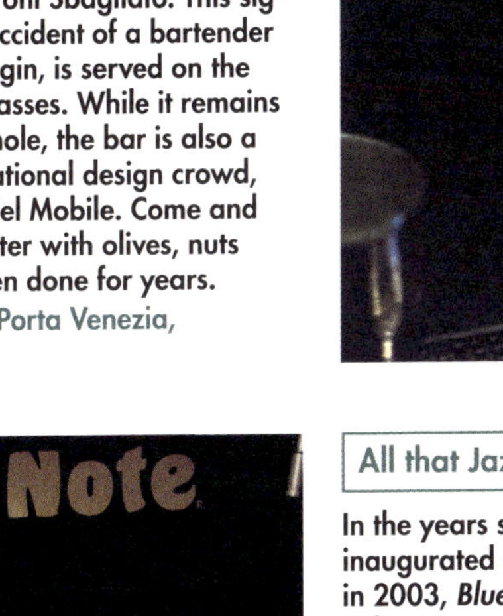

All that Jazz

In the years since jazz legend Chick Corea inaugurated the space with a piano performance in 2003, *Blue Note* has cemented its legacy as Milan's premier jazz venue. Many greats have graced its stage, from Herbie Hancock and Pat Metheny to Joe Lovano and Branford Marsalis, making it a beloved destination for those seeking smooth sounds in a glamorous atmosphere. With a gigantic list of cocktails to choose from, you're sure to find the perfect pairing for the exceptional jazz selections, covering everything from pre-Prohibition to contemporary classics.

• Blue Note Milano, Via Pietro Borsieri 37, Isola, bluenotemilano.com

World's Best Speakeasy

When *1930* opened in 2013, it spread only by whispers. Channeling America's Prohibition era, the speakeasy pairs vintage décor with concept-driven cocktails and bartenders dressed for the part. Now in a new location and ranked on The World's 50 Best Bars, it's still one of Milan's hardest doors to crack. Entry is by invitation only, usually via the bartenders at its sister spot, *MAG la Pusterla*. If you're lucky, you might be led to the basement, and, at the very least, you'll be grateful it's closer than the original Via Sottocorno hideaway.

• 1930, farmilygroup.com, by invitation only

Anna Frabrotta

Analog Dreams

Anna Frabrotta is rewriting the rules of print culture. A journalist and professor of Fashion Publishing at IED Milan, she is also the visionary behind *Frab's Magazines & More*, Italy's first boutique dedicated entirely to independent and collectible magazines. Launched in 2019 as a passion project and online shop, Frab's has grown into a cultural reference point with a flagship in Porta Venezia and a loyal international following. Frabrotta treats each magazine like a work of art, weighing texture, typography and binding as much as the ideas they carry. To her, these aren't just periodicals but "jewels of paper," tactile objects that inspire fresh perspectives and remind us of the sensory power of print in the digital age.

It feels only fitting that Milan, Italy's capital of design, publishing and creativity, should be home to *Frab's Magazines & More*, a sanctuary for indie print. Anna Frabrotta's venue is more than a shop, it's a democratic hub for analog culture, where designers, students and curious readers rediscover the joy of paper. Stocking more than a thousand niche titles, it doubles as a cultural platform, hosting launches, pop-ups and talks. Frabrotta's mission is clear: to elevate independent publishing into an inclusive, sensory-rich experience with global reach.

Égalité
Porta Venezia

Serra di Quartiere
Porta Venezia

loste café
Porta Venezia

Orsonero
Porta Venezia

Pesa Pubblica
Porta Venezia

Bar Picchio
Porta Venezia

Eris
Porta Venezia

Street Food Betlemme
Porta Venezia

Commerce
Porta Venezia

Spazio
Porta Venezia

Bivio
Porta Venezia

You're originally from Molise and later studied in Bologna and Forlì. What eventually brought you to Milan?

Work, partly, but also Milan's soul and creativity. It's Italy's most cosmopolitan city, with the spirit of a European capital and endless opportunities.

Is it an easy city to live in for someone creative?

Yes. Milan recognizes and rewards talent. If you have vision and something meaningful to bring to the table, you can carve out a place here, even without connections.

Tell us more about Frab's. How did it come about and evolve?

I launched Frab's online in 2019 out of a lifelong love for independent magazines. At the time, Italy had no dedicated space for collectible and niche publications, so Frab's set out to fill that gap. It began as an e-commerce platform and soon expanded with shops in Forlì, where I lived, and later in Rome after the pandemic. The amusing part was that people constantly asked where our Milan store was, as if it were obvious we should be there. I eventually took the hint, and in February 2024, we opened in Milan. Today this is our only home, and it makes perfect sense.

Who comes to Frab's?

Our community is wonderfully diverse, from readers who collect for pleasure to designers, fashion insiders and creatives who turn to magazines as a source of constant inspiration. We also host events and talks, which has made us a bit of a cultural reference point in the city.

You're in Porta Venezia. What made you decide to open there?

I love Porta Venezia, so opening in the neighborhood felt completely natural. It's the epicenter of creative Milan, with fashion houses, showrooms, PR agencies and studios all around. Add to that its vibrant nightlife along Via Melzo and Via Lecco and its identity as the city's queer district, which perfectly aligns with our philosophy of openness and with the spirit of many of the magazines we curate.

What are some of your favorite places in the neighborhood?

I'm a breakfast person, so I often indulge at *Égalité* for its impeccable French pastries or at *Serra di Quartiere*, a tiny, cozy café-bistrot. *loste café* and *Orsonero* are also favorites, worth the wait even with the inevitable queue. For aperitivo, I head to *Pesa Pubblica*, while *Bar Picchio* is my go-to for something more low-key. I've also recently discovered *Eris*, a miniscule bar with a refined, minimalist feel that I really like.

And dinner?

Dinner is tough, there are just too many good options in Porta Venezia. One spot I return to often is *Street Food Betlemme*, a Palestinian place that's really, really good.

Are there shops you'd also recommend checking out in the area?

Absolutely. *Commerce* and *Spazio* are two excellent bookshops nearby, with strong focuses on photography and architecture. For vintage fashion, *Bivio* is a must,

A look inside Frab's Magazines & More

Stamberga
Porta Venezia

Seconda Vita Vintage
Porta Venezia

Fairouz
Wagner

Triennale Milano
Parco Sempione

Fondazione Prada
Porta Romana

one of the reasons Milan is such a treasure trove for second-hand finds. *Stamberga* is a real gem for those in search of something special or simply indulging in a bit of dreamy browsing, with its mix of fine stationery, teas from around the world and beautifully curated objects. And for design lovers, *Seconda Vita Vintage* is the spot for distinctive second-hand furnishings.

Any other neighborhoods you love?

Porta Romana for its dining scene, Wagner for its beautiful architecture and the city's best Lebanese spot, *Fairouz*, and Ticinese for its eclectic vibe.

Outside of neighborhoods, what places or institutions inspire you?

The *Triennale* in Parco Sempione. Beyond its excellent exhibitions, it offers talks, concerts, theater and even has a great café and a restaurant with a terrace. It's a place you can experience 360 degrees, and I go often. *Fondazione Prada* is a close second, though a bit harder to reach.

Which Italian indie magazines would you recommend from Frab's shelves?

Cartography, dedicated to travel culture with striking photo essays; *CAP 74024*, a fashion-forward publication; *Lampoon*, which explores culture more broadly; and *Mousse*, known for its critical voices, exhibition reviews, interviews and artist books. They're all based right here in Milan.

Last but not least: How would you describe Milan to someone who's never been here?

I'd say Milan is a city that lives at a fast pace, but it's also full of layers. There's the professional side, the underground energy, which the city's many listening bars capture perfectly, and, of course, its remarkable architecture. It's a multi-faceted place.

A tip for a visitor?

Always look up. Milan's Liberty-style buildings are works of art, and they transform with the light. Pay attention, and you'll see something new each time.

Editors' Picks

Made in Milan

Cultures Crossed

Crafted by the design studio CTRLZAK for Seletti's hybrid collection, this plate blends two distinct cultural aesthetics: the intricate blue and white patterns typical of European bone china and vibrant motifs inspired by Chinese porcelain. This bold juxtaposition creates a unique showpiece that, like Milan itself, symbolizes the fusion of diverse traditions.

• Hybrid, Seletti, seletti.it

Mirror, Mirror, I'm a Star

This mirror, featuring a kaleidoscopic image of hands holding lipsticks, epitomizes the pop art aesthetic of Toiletpaper, a Milanese brand that infuses everyday objects with surreal and subversive imagery. It blurs the line between functional object and visual art, creating an impression that some might interpret as getting the star treatment. To learn more about the brand, see the interview with co-founder Pierpaolo Ferrari in this guide.

• Mirror Gold Frame, shoptoiletpaper.com

The Decanter's Secret

This Ichendorf Milano wine decanter blends functionality with pure imagination. What makes it truly unique is the stationary wine glass that appears to float inside the decanter's tapered body. Serve wine for houseguests, and watch their bewildered faces as the glass slowly merges with each pour. It's a perfect example of how a playful vision and meticulous craftsmanship can turn a regular household object into a surreal statement piece.

• Inbottiglia Wine Decanter Large, ichendorfmilano.com

Books

A Private Venus
• Giorgio Scerbanenco, 1966

Duca Lamberti, a former imprisoned doctor, is hired to straighten out a Milanese mogul's son. That is where the complex ring of prostitution and crime starts. From the father of Italian Noir.

Fiorucci: The Book
• Eve Babitz, Harlin Quist, 1980

A design book about the influential and inspiring brand world of Fiorucci. A true testament to the 1980s fashion scene. A rare find.

Due di due
• Andrea di Carlo, 1989

De Carlo's love-hate relationship with his hometown, Milan, is detailed within his novels. His partially autobiographical book, *Due di due*, is about the friendship between the adventurous and radical Guido and the story's narrator, the more gentle and grounded Mario.

Movies

Milano Calibro 9
• Fernando Di Leo, 1972

The "Mano Armate" genre is characterized by brash, intricately plotted, ultra-violent stories of gangsters, told with attitude and style. These B-movies influenced Tarantino's *Pulp Fiction*.

La Vita Agra
• Carlo Lizzani, 1964

Depicting a revolt against the cultural establishment of 1960s Milan following the Italian economic miracle, this film is based on what is considered one of the most important novels in contemporary Italian literature.

I Am Love
• Luca Guadagnino, 2009

Set in Villa Necchi Campiglio, the plot echoes that of the former owners. The movie, starring Tilda Swinton, is an ostentatious feast with tremendous visual style. A tribute to the conflict between tradition and emotion.

Music

Ennio Morricone Go Jazz
• Jazz Workshop Orchestra & Enrico Intra, 2010

Pianist Enrico Intra is a pioneer in the Italian jazz scene. In 1960 he founded Intra's Derby Club in Milan, where he played together with legends like Chet Baker and Gerry Mulligan. In his collaboration with Jazz Workshop Orchestra, he is performing classics from the Roman soundtrack Maestro.

Mina Live '78
• Mina, 1978

Mina's music is like a good risotto: It touches the soul of everyone, from kids to grandparents. In 1978 the Diva gave her last public concert singing about joy, love and despair, and including an interpretation of Queen's "We Are the Champions" as one of her goodbye tracks. Since then, she has released a new album almost every year.

Leo Mas at Kundula
• Leo Mas, 2014

From Milan to Spain and back, Leo Marras has been one of the protagonists of the Ibiza club scene since the mid '80s. He brought the Italian touch to Balearic Beats and the Summer of Love, and his latest releases, for labels like Italian Records and Polluted, continue along this vibe. His mix for Kundaluna is the perfect sound for a smooth night ride in an Alfa Romeo on Via Gallarate.
Soundcloud.com/leo-mas

THE MYSTERIOUS MAN

By
PALOLO
ROVERSI

FROM THE ORIGINAL TITLE
"MAN OF MYSTERY"

BEST DETECTIVE No. 4 · 25¢
Selection

Observations

The Mysterious Man

Paolo Roversi

The man pushes me, giving me an assassin's glance; a glance full of resentment that will either terrorize you or make you snap like a spring. He doesn't give me time to react, quickly disappearing off the train. I don't even stop to think, instinctively following him to settle the matter. That's how I roll. I have to decide quickly, and I don't hesitate, rushing after him. I have to. Maybe he stole my wallet when he pushed me, but right now, I don't have time to check. I hurry, so as not to lose him, and a thought passes through my mind. The man has a familiar face, but I didn't get a clear enough look at him to be sure.

I follow him up the stairs of the station, crossing piazza Gobetti and onto via Porpora. I know this part of Milan well. It's Lambrate. A city inside the city. A lively area, where journalists, actors, writers and regular Milanese people live alongside immigrants and students. It is evening, and the lights of the street lamps illuminate via Adelchi. I keep walking, ensuring to keep a distance from him.

This area is always vibrant, but it has changed a lot over the last few years. At the end of the '50s, during the economic boom, many large factories were built here. One stands out above the rest, the Innocenti, which produced cars and scooters like the Lambretta, the historic rival of the Vespa. The Lambretta is a part of Milan, but also a part of the world's image of Italy. It was iconic in the American film *Roman Holiday*. Today, the Innocenti factory has closed down, and the workshops have been converted into lofts, art galleries and trendy clubs.

The man has disappeared behind a wood-framed glass door. Above it there is a yellow sign, but I can't read it from where I'm standing. I stop and look around. I have the impression that I'm not alone, as though someone is following me. Is it possible? Yes. I realize it when, from the corner of my eye, I notice a man with a hoodie. He has suddenly appeared behind me with another man, a scarf covering his face. They stare at me insistently, coming towards me from the opposite side of the street.

Who are these people? Maybe I should have let it go, but it's too late now. I'm in for a penny, in for a pound. I push the wooden door open and enter the club. There are a lot of people inside, and in the crowd, I lose sight of the man. He has disappeared, as if swallowed by the whirlpool of people. He reappears, only for an instant. Suddenly, everyone moves aside, leaving a huge empty space at the center of the club where the man stands. He has a knife in his hand; a long, sharp blade. I am about to shout when the lights go out.

Complete blackout. Around me there is only darkness. I'm sweating, breathing with difficulty. I want to back away, but someone grabs me from behind, and I can't move.

The lights suddenly come back on, and there's an explosion of voices and shouts. The knife plunges into an enormous cream cake.

"Happy Birthday!" everyone shouts.

The two strangers have removed their hoods and scarves revealing the faces of my friends, and the mysterious man is the patissier who lives on the floor below me. Even my wife is here, smiling like the Cheshire Cat in the corner of the room, complicit and cunning. I am sure that she is behind everything. I had forgotten it was my birthday today. The surprise worked perfectly, but I was almost scared to death.

Paolo Roversi is a crime fiction writer from Milan. He specializes in "Noir Metropolitano," a subgenre where the plot takes place in cities.

Illustration by Krista Bursey

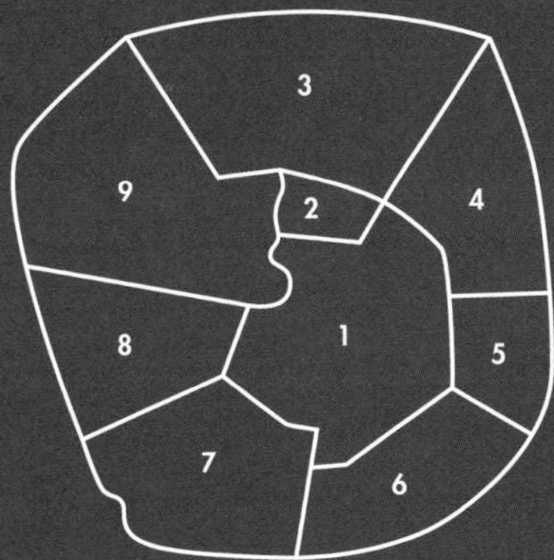

Districts

1 Centro
2 Brera-Garibaldi
3 Isola-Stazione Centrale
4 Porta Venezia
5 Porta Vittoria
6 Porta Romana-Vigentina
7 Navigli-Ticinese
8 San Vittore-Sant'Ambrogio
9 Sempione-Chinatown
0 Outskirts

Ⓒ Culture
Ⓕ Food
Ⓝ Night
◎ Outdoors
Ⓢ Shop

1/Centro

2/Brera-Garibaldi

3/Isola-Stazione Centrale

Osteria dal Verme
Via Jacopo dal Verme, 19
+39 02 6680 2223
osteriadalverme.it
→ p.43 Ⓕ

Ratanà
Via Gaetano de Castillia, 28
+39 02 8712 8855
ratana.it
→ p.6, 23, 44 Ⓕ

Ta-Hua
Via Gustavo Fara, 15
+39 02 4548 8800
tahua.it
→ p.23 Ⓕ

Trattoria da Tomaso
Via Gaetano de Castillia, 20
+39 02 668 8023
trattoriadatomaso.it
→ p.44 Ⓕ

4/Porta Venezia

Bar Basso
Via Plinio, 39
+39 02 2940 0580
barbasso.com
→ p.7, 15, 50 Ⓕ Ⓝ

Bar Picchio
Via Melzo, 11
+39 02 2953 1433
barpicchio.com
→ p.50, 53 Ⓝ

Bivio
Via Lambro, 12
Original + others
+39 02 5810 8691
biviomilano.it
→ p.53 Ⓕ

Casa Capitano
Via Castel Morrone, 35
+39 02 8342 4486
casacapitano.com
→ p.16 Ⓕ

Casa Museo Boschi di Stefano
Via Giorgio Jan, 15
+39 02 8846 4748
casamuseoboschi distefano.it
→ p.15 Ⓒ

Commerce
Via Alessandro Tadino, 30
commerce-commerce .com
→ p.53 Ⓢ

Da Giannino l'Angolo D'Abruzzo
Via Rosolino Pilo, 20
+39 02 2940 6526
da-giannino-langolo -dabruzzo.it
→ p.16 Ⓕ

Égalité
Via Melzo, 22
+39 02 9176 3465
egalitemilano.it
→ p.53 Ⓕ

Eris
Via Bartolomeo Eustachi, 8
+39 02 0996 2094
erismilano.com
→ p.53 Ⓝ

Frab's Magazines & More
Via Giuseppe Sirtori,11
+39 32 9105 2791
frabsmagazines.com
→ p.52 Ⓢ

Galleria d'Arte Moderna (GAM)
Via Palestro, 16
+39 02 8844 5943
gam-milano.com
→ p.19 Ⓒ

Galleria Giò Marconi
Via Alessandro Tadino, 15
+39 02 2940 4373
giomarconi.com
→ p.24 Ⓒ

Giacomo Bistrot
Via Pasquale Sottocorno, 6
+39 02 7602 2653
giacomobistrot.com
→ p.6, 42 Ⓕ Ⓝ

Hostaria Terza Carbonaia
Via degli Scipioni, 3
+39 34 0247 9482
terzacarbonaia.it
→ p.16 Ⓕ

Il Carpaccio
Via Lazzaro Palazzi, 19
+39 02 0995 2990
→ p.16 Ⓕ

L'Antro della Sibilla
Via San Gregorio, 37
+39 02 6748 1054
antrodellasibilla.com
→ p.23 Ⓕ

Le Dictateur
Via Melzo, 34
ledictateurstudio.com
→ p.15 Ⓒ

loste cafe
Via Francesco Guicciardini, 3
+39 02 4537 5475
lostecafe.com
→ p.6, 53 Ⓕ

Massimo De Carlo
Via Privata Giovanni Ventura, 5
Città Studi
+39 02 7000 3987
massimodecarlo.com
→ p.15, 24 Ⓒ

Monica De Cardenas
Via Francesco Viganò, 4
+39 02 2901 0 068
monicadecardenas .com
→ p.24 Ⓒ

Non Solo Lesso
Via Giorgio Jan & Via Francesco Redi
+39 02 3653 3440
nonsololesso.it
→ p.45 Ⓕ

Orsonero
Via Giuseppe Broggi, 15
+39 35 3478 9474
orsonerocoffee.it
→ p.53 Ⓕ

Osteria alla Concorrenza
Via Melzo, 12
+39 02 9167 2012
osteriaallaconcorrenza .superbexperience.com
→ p.50 Ⓕ Ⓝ

PAC Museum
Via Palestro, 14
+39 02 8844 6359
pacmilano.it
→ p.19, 48 Ⓒ

Palazzo Berri-Meregalli
Via Cappuccini, 8
→ p.23 Ⓞ

Pause
Via Federico Ozanam, 7
+39 02 3952 8151
pausemilano.com
→ p.10 Ⓢ

Pavè
Via Felice Casati, 27
+39 02 3790 5491
pavemilano.com
→ p.6, 41 Ⓕ

Pesa Pubblica
Via Melzo, 19
+39 02 4539 7150
pesapubblicamilano.it
→ p.53 Ⓕ

Piccola Ischia
Via Giovanni Battista Morgagni, 7
+39 02 204 7613
piccolaischia.it
→ p.16 Ⓕ

Piscina Cozzi
Viale Tunisia, 35
+39 02 659 9703
→ p.40 Ⓞ

Pizzeria Mundial
Piazza Enrico Bottini, 2
Città Studi
+39 02 7063 7083
→ p.40 Ⓕ

Røst
Via Melzo 3
+39 34 4053 8044
rostmilano.com
→ p.43 Ⓕ

Seconda Vita Vintage
Via Giuseppe Sirtori, 17/19
+39 35 1505 2096
secondavitavintage .com
→ p.55 Ⓢ

Serra di Quartiere
Via Melzo, 3
+39 33 8223 2217
@serradiquartiere
→ p.53 Ⓕ

Spazio
Corso Buenos Aires, 20
+39 02 8353 8119
spaziomilano.org
→ p.53 Ⓢ

Stamberga
Via Gioacchino Rossini, 1
+39 33 5563 6433
stamberga.it
→ p.55 Ⓢ

Street Food Betlemme
Via Panfilo Castaldi, 40
+39 34 7616 3007
→ p.53 Ⓕ

Villa Necchi Campiglio
Via Mozart, 14
+39 02 7634 0121
casemuseomilano.it
→ p.14, 19, 24, 57 Ⓒ

5/Porta Vittoria

Pasticceria Sissi
Piazza Risorgimento, 6
+39 02 7601 4664
→ p.6, 15 Ⓕ

Trattoria del Nuovo Macello
Via. C. Lombroso, 20
+39 02 5990 2122
trattoriadelnuovo macello.it
→ p.7, 44 Ⓕ

6/Porta Romana-Vigentina

Fondazione Prada
L.go Isarco, 2
+39 02 5666 2611
fondazioneprada.org
→ p.48, 55 Ⓒ

Giannasi 1967
Piazza Bruno Buozzi, 2
+39 32 0857 6881
giannasi1967.com
→ p.43 Ⓕ

Un Posto a Milano
Via Privata Cuccagna, 2/4
+39 02 545 7785
unpostoamilano.it
→ p.41 Ⓕ

7/Navigli-Ticinese

1930
Via Edmondo de Amicis, 22
@1930cocktailbar
→ p.51 Ⓕ Ⓝ

Antonioli
Via Pasquale Paoli, 1
+39 02 3656 4834
antonioli.eu
→ p.16 Ⓢ

Frip
Corso di Porta Ticinese, 16
+39 02 8321 3600
frip.it
→ p.16 Ⓢ

Mudec (Museo delle Culture)
Via Tortona, 56
+39 02 54 917
mudec.it
→ p.48 Ⓒ

Nonostante Marras
Via Cola di Rienzo, 8
+39 34 2615 9597
nonostantemarras.it
→ p.10 Ⓢ

WAG
Via Edmondo de Amicis, 28
wagmilano.com
→ p.49 Ⓢ

8/San Vittore-Sant' Ambrogio

Fairouz
Via Michelangelo Buonarroti, 16
+39 02 481 8331
Original in Wagner + other others
fairouzmilano.com
→ p.55 Ⓕ

Galleria Rossana Orlandi
Via Matteo Bandello, 14
+39 02 467 4471
rossanaorlandi.com
→ p.24, 41 ⒸⓈ

MAG la Pusterla
Via Edmondo de Amicis, 22
+39 02 4975 5094
farmilygroup.com
→ p.51 Ⓕ Ⓝ

Museo del Archeologico
Corso Magenta, 15
+39 02 8844 5208
museoarcheologicom-ilano.it
→ p.48 Ⓒ

Museo della Scienza e della Tecnologia
Via San Vittore, 21
+39 02 485 551
museoscienza.org
→ p.48 Ⓒ

9/Sempione-Chinatown

Fondazione Achille Castiglioni
Piazza Castello, 27
+39 2805 3606
achillecastiglioni.it
→ p.19 Ⓒ

Archivio Farini
Via Giulio Cesare Procaccini, 4
+39 02 6680 4473
viafarini.org
→ p.15 Ⓒ

Fabbrica del Vapore
Via Giulio Cesare Procaccini, 4
+39 38 9650 4494
fabbricadelvapore .org
→ p.48 Ⓒ

Luisa delle Piane
Via Giuseppe Giusti, 24
+39 02 331 9680
gallerialuisadelle piane.it
→ p.24 Ⓒ

Ravioleria Sarpi
Via Paolo Sarpi, 27
+39 331 887 0596
laravioleriasarpi.com
→ p.9 Ⓕ

Long Chang
Via Paolo Sarpi, 42
+39 02 331 1098
trattorialongchang.com
→ p.40 Ⓕ

Triennale di Milano
Viale Alemagna,6
+39 02 72 4341
triennale.org
→ p.24, 41, 48 Ⓝ Ⓞ

0/Outskirts

Astrofat
Piazzale Giovanni delle Bande Nere, 9
+39 02 4975 5722
astrofat.it
→ p.49 Ⓢ

ONEOFF
Via Guido Capelli, 12
+39 02 3651 7890
oneoff.it
→ p.40 Ⓒ

Pirelli HangarBicocca
Via Chiese, 2
+39 02 6611 1573
hangarbicocca.org
→ p.41, 48 Ⓒ

The Amazing Art
Parco del Polifunzio-nale in Via Gramsci 31
theamazingart.com
→ p.48, 49 Ⓒ

Upcycle
Via A. M. Ampère, 59
+39 02 8342 8268
upcyclecafe.it
→ p.41 Ⓕ

JOIN THE ONES WHO DO MORE
THAN JUST VISIT CITIES
LOSTIN
SCAN THE CODE, BECOME
A LOST IN MEMBER, AND
NEVER MISS OUT
LOSTiN